BISEXUAL HEALTH

UNDERSTANDING UNIQUE CHALLENGES, NEEDS, AND WELLNESS STRATEGIES

DR. J.P JUDE

Contents

CHAPTER ONE

INTRODUCTION

People who identify as bisexual—that is, who are attracted to both men and women—and their physical, mental, emotional, and social well-being are all included in the category of bisexual health. Social attitudes, stigma, and misperceptions about bisexuality might provide particular health issues and experiences for bisexual people. Promoting inclusivity, reducing inequities, and guaranteeing fair access to healthcare for bisexual people all depend on an understanding of bisexual health.

Important Factors in the Health of Bisexuals:

Sexual Wellness:

Safe Sex Practices: Since bisexual people may have sex with people of multiple genders, they should have access to resources for safe sex practices, such as barrier techniques and condoms, as well as complete sexual health education.

Frequent testing: Maintaining sexual health and well-being requires routine testing for HIV, STIs, and other sexual health issues.

Mental Wellness:

Mental Health Risks: Because of their experiences with stigma, discrimination, and minority stress, bisexual people may be more susceptible to mental health problems such as depression, anxiety, and suicide thoughts.

Access to Mental Health Services: Treating mental health issues and fostering wellbeing depend on having readily available, culturally sensitive mental health services that affirm and support bisexual identities.

Physical Condition:

Frequent Check-ups: Preventive care, screenings, and physical examinations are crucial for preserving general health and spotting possible hazards or issues.

Chronic Conditions: There may be differences in the frequency and treatment of chronic conditions among bisexual people, which highlights the need for early detection and focused interventions.

Community & Social Support:

Social Support: Creating networks and communities of support can help lessen the negative impacts of discrimination, stigma, and exclusion while also offering bisexual people important support and affirmation.

Advocacy & Visibility: Increasing bisexual visibility, awareness, and advocacy can help dispel stigma, dispel misconceptions, and create a more accepting and affirming community.

Cultural Proficiency and Broad Inclusion:

Healthcare Professionals: on order to treat bisexual people with respect, affirmation, and complete care, healthcare professionals should undergo training on bisexual health, cultural competency, and LGBTQ+ inclusive care.

Healthcare Settings: Better patient-provider communication, health outcomes, and access to care can all be achieved by establishing inclusive healthcare environments that accept and celebrate a range of sexual orientations and gender identities.

Bisexual health is a complicated and multidimensional topic that needs for thorough knowledge, awareness, and assistance. We may endeavor to promote holistic well-being, lessen health disparities, and create inclusive environments that support and celebrate bisexual identities by acknowledging the distinct experiences, difficulties, and needs of bisexual people.

Bisexual health must be prioritized and promoted by healthcare professionals, legislators, educators, community leaders, and allies in research, policy creation, healthcare delivery, and community initiatives. By working together, we can build a culture and healthcare system that are more equal, accepting, and affirming of every person, regardless of their sexual orientation or identity.

Comprehending the Identity of Bisexuals

Recognizing and appreciating the diversity, fluidity, and complexity of sexual orientation is essential to understanding bisexual identity. Although individuals who identify as bisexual may also be attracted to people of other genders, bisexuality is defined as a sexual orientation marked by emotional, romantic, or sexual attraction to both men and women. Bisexual identity is a continuum that includes a vast array of experiences, emotions, and manifestations.

Important Bisexual Identity Factors:

Draw:

Dual Attraction: Although the degree and type of this attraction can differ greatly amongst individuals, bisexuals are attracted to both men and women.

Fluidity: A dynamic and ever-evolving understanding of one's sexual orientation is made possible by the fluidity of bisexual attraction, which can fluctuate over time.

Behavior versus Sexual Orientation:

Differentiation: behavior is what a person does as a result of their activities, but sexual orientation is their innate attraction to other people. Attraction, not necessarily conduct or relationships, is what defines a bisexual identity.

Versatility: Bisexual attraction is inclusive and versatile, as demonstrated by the fact that bisexual individuals can form relationships with individuals of any gender.

Affirmation and Visibility:

Underrepresentation: Due to social prejudices, misunderstandings, and bisexual erasure, bisexual people may experience difficulties with visibility, representation, and identity recognition.

Visibility Matters: By promoting and supporting bisexual identities via advocacy, representation, and visibility, we may dispel stigma, dispel misconceptions, and promote a more accepting view of bisexuality.

Cross-sectionality:

Many identities: Bisexual people may have intersecting identities with respect to gender, color, class, disability, and other social issues.

These identities can have an impact on their experiences, difficulties, and viewpoints.

Complexity and variety: Acknowledging the intersectional character of bisexual identification draws attention to the community's complexity and variety, highlighting the significance of inclusive and culturally sensitive methods for comprehending and assisting bisexual people.

Confirmation & Validation:

Acknowledgment: Bisexual people can be empowered, their well-being improved, and a sense of acceptance and belonging can be fostered by validating and affirming their bisexual identities through courteous language, inclusive policies, and friendly surroundings.

Displacing Myths and Stereotypes: Dispelling myths, prejudices, and false beliefs about bisexuality through factual knowledge, awareness, and education helps lessen stigma and foster acceptance.

A nuanced, inclusive approach that acknowledges the range, complexity, and validity of bisexual experiences is necessary to understand bisexual identity. A valid and normal sexual orientation, bisexuality adds to the rich fabric of human expression and variation. We can build more inclusive, courteous, and supportive environments that celebrate the full range of human sexuality and promote well-being for all persons, regardless of their sexual orientation or identity, by promoting knowledge, education, acceptance, and affirmation of bisexual identities.

Health Inequalities and Obstacles

Bisexual people frequently have particular health inequalities and difficulties as a result of culturally competent treatment being scarce, prejudice, and societal stigma. The physical, mental, emotional, and social well-being of bisexual people can be significantly impacted by these differences, underscoring the necessity of focused interventions, welcoming policies, and encouraging surroundings.

Health Inequalities:

Mental Wellness:

Greater Frequencies of Mental Health Problems: When compared to their heterosexual and homosexual counterparts, bisexual people may be more likely to suffer from depression, anxiety, suicidal thoughts, and other mental health issues.

Minority Stress: Bisexuality-related experiences of stigma, discrimination, and minority stress can exacerbate psychological discomfort and inequities in mental health.

Sexual Wellness:

HIV and STIs: Bisexual people may be more susceptible to HIV and STIs as a result of a variety of sexual relationships, a lack of sexual health education, and obstacles to receiving resources and services for prevention.

CHAPTER TWO

Safe Sex Practices: Open discussion about sexual health with partners and healthcare providers may be hampered by misconceptions, stigma, and lack of awareness regarding bisexuality.

Physical Condition:

Chronic Conditions: There may be differences in the incidence, treatment, and prognosis of bisexual people for chronic illnesses such as cancer, heart disease, and other ailments.

Healthcare Access: Disparities in physical health outcomes may be caused by obstacles to receiving high-quality healthcare, such as financial constraints, discrimination, and a lack of inclusive treatment.

Use of Substances:

Greater Rates of Substance Use: When compared to heterosexual and gay people, bisexual people may use tobacco, alcohol, and drugs at higher rates. This can lead to a number of health concerns and issues.

Coping Mechanism: Using drugs or alcohol to cope with stress, prejudice, and minority stress associated with bisexuality is possible.

Victimization and Violence:

Increased Risks: Because bisexual people may be more likely to encounter violence, victimization, and intimate partner violence, it's important to provide them with safety, support, and intervention programs that are specific to their needs.

Problems:

Stigma and Prejudice:

Internalized Stigma: Shame, loneliness, and the hiding of one's bisexual identity can result from internalized biphobia and stigma, which can affect one's self-worth, identity formation, and general well-being.

Systemic Discrimination: In the healthcare, workplace, and social contexts, systemic discrimination, heteronormativity, and biphobia can erect obstacles in the way of acceptance, inclusion, and access to services and assistance.

Absence of Knowledge and Inquiry:

Limited Resources: Misconceptions, misinformation, and a lack of understanding regarding bisexuality among healthcare professionals, educators, legislators, and the general public can be caused by the limited availability of bisexual-specific resources, information, and education.

Cultural Competency: Insufficient instruction and knowledge regarding bisexual health, cultural competency, and LGBTQ+ inclusive care may impede the successful diagnosis, treatment, and provision of support for bisexual people.

Access to and Quality of Healthcare:

Inequitable Care: Bisexual people's health and well-being may be jeopardized by unequal access to high-quality healthcare, a dearth of services catering to their needs, and their experiences with prejudice and microaggressions in medical settings.

Effectively addressing the multiple, intricate, and linked issues of bisexual health disparities and challenges calls for comprehensive tactics, advocacy, and teamwork. It is imperative to give bisexual health top priority in research, policy formation, education, and healthcare delivery in order to minimize inequalities, advance equity, and create welcoming environments that embrace, support, and celebrate bisexual identities.

We can work toward creating a more equitable, inclusive, and affirming society that honors and values the health and well-being of bisexual individuals and ensures they have equal opportunities for living healthy, fulfilling lives free from discrimination and prejudice by increasing awareness, challenging stigma, advocating for inclusive policies, improving cultural competency, and offering targeted resources and support.

Obstacles to Healthcare Utilization and Access

Bisexual individuals often confront numerous barriers to accessing and utilizing healthcare services, contributing to disparities in health outcomes and well-being. These obstacles may originate from societal perceptions, systemic problems, ignorance, and a lack of cultural competency in healthcare environments. Improving bisexual people's access to, and results from, healthcare requires an understanding of and commitment to resolving these obstacles.

Obstacles to Obtaining and Using Healthcare:

Discrimination as well as Shame:

Prejudice and Bias: Bisexual people may encounter prejudice, heteronormativity, and biphobia in medical settings, which can result in unfavorable encounters, a reluctance to seek care, and a refusal to use healthcare services.

Microaggressions: Insensitive comments, assumptions about bisexuality, and other subtle types of discrimination can create circumstances that are unwelcoming and invalidating, which discourages bisexual people from seeking care.

Absence of Affirmative and Inclusive Care:

Cultural Competency: Healthcare providers may provide insufficient, ignorant, or insensitive care that ignores the special needs and experiences of bisexual people due to a lack of knowledge, comprehension, and training regarding bisexual health, cultural competency, and LGBTQ+ inclusive care.

Inclusive Policies and Practices: In the absence of affirming practices, nondiscrimination protections, and inclusive policies, bisexual patients may feel excluded, mistrusted, and unsatisfied in healthcare settings.

Budgetary Obstacles:

Insurance Coverage: Bisexual people may find it more difficult to receive necessary healthcare services if their insurance does not provide enough coverage for gender-affirming care, LGBTQ+ inclusive services, or preventive screenings.

Cost Concerns: Bisexual people may be discouraged from obtaining critical medical care, treatments, and prescriptions due to budgetary restrictions, out-of-pocket payments, and affordability concerns.

Absence of Knowledge and Inquiry:

Limited Resources: Misconceptions, misinformation, and a lack of awareness regarding bisexual health needs, risks, and recommendations can arise from the absence of bisexual-specific resources, information, and education available to healthcare professionals and patients.

Patient Education: Insufficient, customized patient education and resources might hinder bisexual people's ability to make educated decisions, be medically literate, and advocate for themselves.

Barriers based on geography and structure:

Accessibility: There may be logistical obstacles and impediments to receiving timely and adequate care due to geographic location, transportation concerns, and a lack of healthcare facilities, services, and providers who specialize in bisexual health.

Systemic Inequities: Health disparities among bisexual people can be exacerbated by structural impediments associated with systemic inequities, socioeconomic disparities, and social determinants of health.

In order to effectively address the obstacles that bisexual people confront while accessing and using healthcare, a multimodal strategy that includes systemic adjustments, legislative changes, community involvement, education, and lobbying is needed. To create more inclusive, accessible, and equitable healthcare environments for bisexual people, it is imperative to prioritize LGBTQ+ inclusive care, promote cultural competency, implement affirming policies and practices, expand insurance coverage, raise awareness and educate the public, and address systemic inequities.

Healthcare professionals, organizations, legislators, and advocates can collaborate to improve bisexual people's access to, and outcomes from, healthcare by identifying and actively removing these barriers. This will guarantee that these people receive patient-centered, affirming, and courteous care that respects and supports their individual identities, experiences, and needs.

Methods for Enhancing the Health of Bisexuals

A thorough, multifaceted strategy that tackles structural obstacles, encourages inclusivity, and creates a nurturing atmosphere for bisexual people is needed to improve bisexual health. Reducing inequities, improving access to healthcare, and promoting bisexual people's well-being can all be achieved through the implementation of focused methods in the fields of healthcare, education, policy, and community settings. Here are some tactics to think about:

Healthcare Systems and Providers:

Training in Cultural Competence:

Continually educate medical professionals about bisexual health, cultural sensitivity, LGBTQ+ inclusive care, and how to deal with prejudice, stigma, and discrimination.

Including Practices and Policies:

Adopt and uphold inclusive language, affirming behaviors, and nondiscrimination rules that honor and support bisexual identities and experiences.

Patient-First Healthcare:

Encourage a patient-centered approach that places a high value on courteous, affirming interactions with bisexual patients, open communication, educated decision-making, and shared decision-making.

Both affordability and accessibility:

Increase the availability of services for bisexuals, treatment that is gender affirming, resources for sexual health, screenings for prevention, and mental health assistance.

To alleviate financial obstacles and improve affordability, support insurance policies, financial aid initiatives, and sliding-scale prices.

CHAPTER THREE

Knowledge and Consciousness:

Campaigns for Public Awareness:

Create and disseminate campaigns, instructional materials, and other tools to combat stigma, dispel misconceptions, and increase public knowledge about bisexuality and bisexual health.

Education in Schools:

Incorporate thorough, LGBTQ+ inclusive sexual health education programs into school curricula to support bisexual students' wellbeing, disseminate accurate information, and encourage healthy relationships.

Community Engagement and Outreach:

To give bisexual people and their families information, resources, and support, get involved with community organizations, LGBTQ+ centers, support groups, and advocacy networks.

Advocacy and Policy:

Reforms in Policy:

Encourage the passage of laws, rules, and policy changes that uphold and advance the rights of bisexual people, healthcare equity, anti-discrimination laws, and inclusive healthcare practices.

Investigation and Gathering of Data:

In order to educate policy, practice, and advocacy efforts, support and fund research initiatives, studies, and data gathering efforts that center on bisexual health inequalities, outcomes, needs, and experiences.

Support and Community:

Conducive Conditions:

Establish welcoming, affirming environments and locations that encourage connection, validation, and support for bisexual people and supporters. Examples of these include social networks, LGBTQ+ community centers, and support groups.

Peer Guidance and Mentoring:

Create leadership development programs, mentorship opportunities, and peer support systems that empower bisexual people, encourage resiliency, and strengthen community capacity.

It takes a team effort from healthcare professionals, educators, legislators, community leaders, advocates, and allies to improve bisexual health. We can work together to create a more inclusive, equitable, and affirming society that respects, values, and supports the health and well-being of bisexual people by putting these strategies into practice, encouraging collaboration, and giving bisexual health top priority in research, policy, education, and healthcare delivery.

Bisexual voices must be heard, their experiences must be prioritized, and they must be included as participants in identifying problems, creating solutions, and enacting change. By working together, we can break down barriers, raise awareness, fight for justice, and create a more positive and healthy future free from stigma, prejudice, and inequality for all bisexual people.

Safer Sexual Practices and Sexual Health

The physical, emotional, mental, and social facets of sexuality are all included in sexual health, which is a crucial aspect of general wellbeing. Like everyone else, bisexual people gain from having access to tools, thorough sexual health education, and support in order to make decisions regarding their sexual health and well-being. Reducing the incidence of unplanned pregnancies and sexually transmitted infections (STIs), such as HIV, requires safer sexual behaviors. This is a bisexual-specific guide to safer sexual practices and sexual health:

Education on Sexual Health:

Entire Sexual Education Program:

Encourage the implementation of thorough, LGBTQ+-inclusive sexual health education programs that address a variety of issues, such as consent, gender identity, sexual orientation, safer sexual practices, contraception, and STI prevention.

Resources That Are Easy to Access:

Provide bisexual people with resources, information, and tools related to sexual health that are inclusive, accurate, and accessible while taking into account their particular needs, worries, and experiences.

safer sexual behavior

Use of Condoms:

Regular Use: Using condoms appropriately during oral, anal, and vaginal sex can cut the risk of STIs, including HIV, dramatically.

Lubrication: To lessen friction, improve comfort, and lower the chance of condom breakage, use silicone- or water-based lubricants with condoms.

Frequent Examinations and Screenings:

STI Testing: Early detection, treatment, and prevention of HIV, gonorrhea, chlamydia, syphilis, and other STIs depend on routine STI testing and screenings.

Communicating openly with partners about sexual health, testing, and STI status can promote transparency, trust, and cooperative decision-making about safer sexual behaviors.

Prophylaxis before exposure (PrEP):

HIV Prevention: For those at high risk of HIV infection, such as bisexuals who have several partners or partners who are HIV-positive, PrEP is a daily medicine that can lower the risk of HIV transmission.

Access and Support: To maximize PrEP's efficacy and handle any possible side effects, make sure you have access to regular monitoring, follow-up care, and support services.

Sexual Health Examinations:

Complete Care: Make an appointment for routine sexual health examinations with medical professionals who are familiar with bisexual health issues. They can talk about past sexual experiences, evaluate risks, offer counseling, and administer preventive care and immunizations (such as the HPV vaccine).

Family planning and birth control:

Contraception: To avoid unwanted pregnancies and support reproductive choices, learn about and have a conversation about contraceptive alternatives, including oral contraceptives, intrauterine devices (IUDs), implants, and other techniques.

Emergency Contraception: To lower the risk of pregnancy, be aware of emergency contraceptive choices, such as Plan B, to use after unprotected intercourse.

Consent and Communication:

Honest Communication

Talk About Boundaries: Be honest and open with your partners about your expectations, preferences, and boundaries when it comes to safer sexual practices, consent, and sexual activities.

Assent:

Get and honor mutual consent before having sex, making sure that both partners voluntarily and voluntarily consent to the activity.

Encourage knowledge, understanding, and communication around respect, boundaries, affirmative sexual experiences, and consent in partnerships and interactions.

For bisexual people, maintaining their general well-being and taking care of themselves requires promoting sexual health and engaging in safer sexual behavior. Bisexual people can make educated decisions, lower risks, and improve their sexual health and well-being by emphasizing thorough sexual health education, resource accessibility, supportive healthcare services, and open communication about safer sex practices.

The needs, rights, and dignity of bisexual people with regard to their sexual health are greatly supported by inclusive, affirming, and accessible environments that are created by healthcare professionals, educators, legislators, community organizations, and activists. By working together, we can enable bisexual people to take control of their sexual well-being, cultivate wholesome relationships, and have satisfying, secure, and enjoyable sex.

A vital component of total well-being, mental health includes social, psychological, and emotional facets of life. Because of societal stigma, discrimination, minority stress, and other issues connected to their sexual orientation, bisexual people may experience particular mental health difficulties. It is essential to recognize and address these issues if we are to support bisexual people's resilience, mental health, and general well-being. This is a bisexual-specific guide to mental health and well-being:

Challenges related to mental health:

Discrimination and Stress Among Minorities:

Stigma and Discrimination: Bisexual people may encounter stigma, prejudice, biphobia, and discrimination in a variety of contexts, such as the medical field, the job, educational institutions, and local communities. This can result in heightened levels of stress, anxiety, and psychological discomfort.

Internalized Biphobia: Holding onto unfavorable views and prejudices about bisexuality from society can have a detrimental effect on one's identity, self-worth, and mental health. It can also lead to feelings of shame, loneliness, and concealment of one's bisexual identity.

CHAPTER FOUR

Disorders of the Mind:

Greater Rates of Disorders: Compared to heterosexual and homosexual people, bisexual people may have greater rates of mental health conditions, such as depression, anxiety disorders, suicidal thoughts, drug use disorders, and post-traumatic stress disorder (PTSD).

Complex Interplay: Bisexual people may have complex mental health needs and experiences as a result of the interaction of their sexual orientation, gender identity, prejudice, trauma, and other variables.

Social and Interpersonal Difficulties:

Relationship Stress: Bisexual people may experience difficulties in their relationships with spouses, families, friends, and the community, such as acceptance, communication, and support issues. These difficulties can have an adverse effect on their mental health and general wellbeing.

Social Isolation: Social ties, support systems, and mental health outcomes can all be impacted by feelings of loneliness, isolation, and a lack of belonging brought on by one's status as a minority, by being invisible, or by rejection.

Techniques for Optimal Mental Health and Wellness:

Care That Is Culturally Competent:

Affirming and Inclusive Services: Offer mental health services that are inclusive, affirming, and culturally competent while also recognizing and validating the particular needs, experiences, and worries of bisexual people.

Provide LGBTQ+-affirmative counseling, therapy, and support groups with a focus on bisexual issues, identity development, coming out, relationship difficulties, and mental health issues.

Conducive Conditions:

Community Support: Encourage the creation of welcoming, affirming spaces for bisexual people and allies, such as social networks, LGBTQ+ community centers, and support groups. These spaces offer bisexual people and allies a sense of belonging, validation, and peer support.

Safe Spaces: Arrange activities, events, and safe spaces that honor bisexuality, increase visibility, dispel preconceptions, and strengthen relationships to the local community.

Knowledge and Consciousness:

Mental Health Literacy: Raise public knowledge and understanding of bisexual mental health, minority stress, coping mechanisms, self-care, resilience, and the resources and support services that are accessible.

Advocacy and Visibility: To combat stigma, increase understanding and support, and raise awareness, advocate for bisexual representation, visibility, and inclusion in mental health programs, research, and policy creation.

Self-Management and Coping Techniques:

Self-Compassion and Acceptance: To promote resilience, mental and emotional health, and a good self-image and identity, practice self-compassion, acceptance, self-care, and self-acceptance.

Healthy Coping Mechanisms: To manage stress, improve coping abilities, and foster general well-being, investigate and participate in healthy coping mechanisms, stress reduction strategies, mindfulness exercises, hobbies, physical activities, and supportive relationships.

Participation in Community and Advocacy:

Empowerment and Leadership: Give bisexual people the tools they need to take up leadership roles, participate in community involvement, advocacy, and activism in order to fight for their rights, advance social justice, and bring about good changes in both their local communities and society as a whole.

Encouraging bisexual people's mental health and well-being calls for an all-encompassing, caring, and cooperative strategy that tackles structural obstacles, cultivates encouraging surroundings, and gives people the confidence to ask for support, connection, and assistance when they need it. We can all work together to improve the mental health, resilience, and quality of life for bisexual people by placing a high priority on self-care, education, advocacy, and culturally competent care.

In order to create inclusive, affirming, and easily available mental health support systems and services, it is imperative that healthcare practitioners, mental health experts, educators, legislators, community groups, allies, and bisexual individuals themselves take on crucial responsibilities. By working together, we can create a culture that is more understanding, kind, and supportive of one another as well as one that respects and cherishes everyone's mental health and wellbeing, regardless of their sexual orientation or identity.

Drug Use and Reduction of Harm

Bisexual people's health, happiness, and quality of life can all be significantly impacted by substance abuse and the hazards that go along with it. Stigma, discrimination, stress related to being a minority, mental health conditions, and social isolation are some of the factors that might lead to an increase in substance use among bisexual people. It is possible to reduce hazards and encourage safer, healthier choices by putting harm reduction measures into practice and by offering helpful resources. This is a bisexual-specific guide to understanding substance use and harm reduction:

Problems with Substance Abuse:

Greater Substance Use Rates:

Increased Risk: Compared to heterosexual and homosexual people, bisexual people may use tobacco, alcohol, and drugs at higher rates. This can result in a number of health risks and difficulties.

Co-occurring Conditions:

Mental Health and Substance Abuse: When mental health conditions like PTSD, depression, or anxiety coexist with drug abuse, it can lead to complicated issues that affect recovery from treatment and general well-being.

Coping Strategies:

Stress and Coping: Using drugs or alcohol as a coping method for bisexuality-related stress, discrimination, minority stress, and other difficulties can lead to addiction, dependence, and health problems.

Strategies for Reducing Harm:

Knowledge and Consciousness:

Enable bisexual people to make well-informed decisions about their health and well-being by promoting education, awareness, and knowledge on the dangers, impacts, and repercussions of substance use as well as harm reduction techniques and resources.

Improved Safety:

Reducing hazards: To reduce harm, hazards, and unfavorable outcomes, promote safer usage methods, moderation, and responsible substance intake, including alcohol, tobacco, and narcotics.

Safe Consumption Kits: To lower the dangers connected with substance use, make safe consumption kits, harm reduction supplies (such as clean needles and naloxone kits), and information on safer use practices accessible.

Obtaining Assistance and Provisions:

Supportive Resources: Provide bisexual people with access to programs, services, and resources that are specifically designed to meet their unique needs and experiences. These programs may include peer support, drug abuse treatment, counseling, harm reduction, and recovery support.

Social Involvement and Peer Assistance:

Peer-Led efforts: Encourage and support community-based programs, support groups, and peer-led harm reduction efforts that provide bisexual people with substance use disorders with a sense of belonging, validation, and peer support.

Policy Promotion:

Advocate for laws, rules, and policies that encourage harm reduction strategies, decriminalize drug use, increase access to treatment and support services, and advance fairness for bisexual people in the medical field and in social services.

An strategy that is compassionate, nonjudgmental, and collaborative is necessary to address substance use and promote harm reduction among bisexual individuals. This approach should prioritize education, awareness, support, and resource accessibility. We can collaborate to lower risks, increase safety, and promote the health and well-being of bisexual people affected by substance use by putting harm reduction ideas into practice, creating supportive environments, and campaigning for legislative changes.

The development of inclusive, accessible, and successful harm reduction programs, services, and policies involves the collaboration of healthcare practitioners, mental health experts, drug abuse specialists, educators, legislators, community organizations, and activists. By working together, we can enable bisexual people to make better decisions, get the help they require, and lead happy, drug-free lives that respect and value their potential, well-being, and dignity.

Summary

In conclusion, a comprehensive strategy that takes into account the physical, mental, and social aspects of well-being is needed to address the particular health issues that bisexual people experience. Reducing inequities, increasing equity, and improving overall health outcomes require an understanding of the complexity of bisexual identity, support for inclusive policies, and friendly surroundings.

Bisexual people's lives can be greatly improved by giving priority to comprehensive treatment, education, and resources catered to their needs. These services might range from safer sexual practices and sexual health to mental health and substance abuse. Bisexual people must be given more power, have their views heard, and be included as partners in their care as well as in the creation of policies and initiatives that impact their health and wellbeing.

In order to build a culture that is more welcoming, affirming, and equal, healthcare professionals, legislators, educators, community leaders, supporters, and bisexual people themselves all play critical roles. We can create a more promising future where everyone, regardless of sexual orientation or identity, has the chance to live healthy, meaningful lives free from stigma, discrimination, and inequalities by cooperating, advocating, and working together.

When we work together, we can change things for the better, promote understanding, and bring about constructive change that values and celebrates the wide range of identities and experiences that people have. To create a more compassionate and welcoming society for all, let's keep learning, developing, and evolving in our knowledge of and support for the health, rights, and well-being of bisexual people.

THE END